Eternal Echoes

Also by Jay Long

Timeless Chatter
Between the Heart and Mind

Eternal Echoes

a collection of poetry and prose by

Jay Long

300 South Media Group
New York

Eternal Echoes

Copyright © 2017 by Jay Long

All rights reserved.

Book design by 300 South Media Group
300SMG.com

No part of this book may be reproduced in any form or by any electronic or mechanical means including information storage and retrieval systems, without permission in writing from the author. The only exception is for book reviews or articles written about the book and/or author.

For licensing or copyright information
please contact info@300smg.com

This book is presented as a collection.

Jay Long
Visit the website jaylongwrites.com

Printed in the United States of America

ISBN-13: 978-0-9970356-2-9

For those who **share the rhetoric** every day, your wildest dreams have no boundaries.

Eternal Echoes

INTRODUCTION

We all travel along similar paths through life. Words and writing connect us as we relate our own journeys to that of the writer. Poetry, more so than other forms of writing, lets us know, no matter what, 'I am not alone' and 'everything will be OK'. Readers connect to the poet and on some level, the two become intimate partners, even if for a short time. Eternal Echoes is a collection of writings that brings the reader along a journey into a deeper aspect of the writer's soul. There's love and loss as well as motivation, inspiration, and an overall acceptance of life's journey and how those moments, are much more important than the destination.

Eternal Echoes

Eternal Echoes

Her touch felt like fireflies jumping across my
 back
The sparkle in her eyes set fire to the wind
The inviting softness of her mouth held every
 love song ever written
And her laughter is sure to echo for eternity

Bloodlines

I was not cut from any cloth.
I was put together with the
ripped and shredded scraps
of those that came before me.
My stitching is made of gold
and I will never fray.

Whiskey Veins

There's whiskey in her veins
and each new day is like my happy hour.
I raise my glass to the man I am with her.
The sound of her voice
leaves me drunk with passion
and I cannot wait for the next sip.

A Moment in Time

Had I known the curtain would fall before the
final act
I would have run through the aisles during
intermission
Spreading my love for you like confetti on New
Year's Eve
I' would have grabbed every noise maker
and started a seventy-two-piece band
Played on the corner of Broadway and 7th Avenue
Humming out a love song on my kazoo
As the world got a little older, and life got a little
colder
Now with every second that ticks
The ball freezes in time
A toast to you dear friend
I will celebrate your life
From this day until my last
With drug store champagne and cheap plastic
glasses

Tracks

Her weary bones seemed to break in place
as they wrapped around me from behind.
Her long-lost gray eyes filled with joy
when she saw the smile across my face welcoming her home.
The wishes of endless days
had finally found their way
and I could feel her heart beat
as if it were an out of control freight train
laying its own tracks.

Demon Dance

I feel for those that have never been kept awake all night by the thoughts that run around in the darkness..the ghosts that bring back memories or the demons that dance beside the fire. How boring their lives must be.

Until Then

You taught me to live
To choose my path without regrets
That with a pure heart
Anything is possible
From now until then
I will forever believe
We leave this world
When our task is done
I wonder if you see me
Do the clouds really have holes
Is your watchful eye my guiding light
Or have the heavens taken that too?

Smile Shines

Just yesterday you walked into my life and shared a moment. And when I look back on it all, I'll sit and remember that somewhere between the first and last day, a smile shined and I fell in love.

The Edge

here we are once again
standing on the doorstep of perfection
it's all too familiar
the night
the silence
us against the world

we have been here far too many times
to know it will all be alright
in an instant, it can all be taken away
the excitement
the hope
a lifetime of disappointment

when the lights go down
no one can say we didn't give our all
we left everything on the table
the promises
the dreams
our chance to make it last

Paper and Pen

I long for the day that I can look at letters and not feel the need to unscramble them into stories of uncommon love. I see the stars and for a brief moment, I wish that each one would shoot across the sky bringing hope to broken souls. I bet on long shots because I know magic can happen in an instant. Kisses can break down walls even the heaviest of burdens have built. I smile at the thought that the spark of true love can be ignited by the simple twinkle of an eye and how a lifetime can be lived in a shared moment.

Just Dessert

The way her name rolls off my tongue and over my lips, it fills my mouth like my favorite dessert and I can't wait to taste her, over and over again.

Sunshine Deja Vu

Her eyes blinked in the sunshine as golden rays of happiness struck her face and framed my future. Like a sudden deja vu, I felt as if I'd been
here before.
My name sounded just like a song when it escaped her lips.
The beat of her heart echoed out like
a warrior's call; as if the heavens were sent to summon my destiny.
There are no shattered pieces of the past, no blind promise of tomorrow, just living one today at a time.

Tea Party

The scream of my heart beat seems to scare away the ghosts in the night. The clown that hangs in the corner of the room no longer frowns with fear but smiles with insane happiness. The demons that made their home under the bed have joined me between the sheets and we enjoy an afternoon tea party each Friday now that you're gone.

The Open Book

Here I am searching for the next piece of inspiration.
Dreaming of the movie my life would
make.
The love song I'd sing for my other half.
The dust pile I'll be sweeping when it's over.
The empty hand I'll be left holding at the end of the day.
My soul is an open book;
'A fool and his heart',
a best seller about being young and free and growing old
with restless wings that let me soar.

So many sit back and accept the actions of others.
Tolerance speaks much louder than words. Let the heart
realize it's worth. Never beg to be loved.

Homecoming

Her mind was quiet
The only sound was that of the rain
It came down sideways
Reminded her of being a child
Riding the swings at the fair
How her feet dangled
Her hair tousled in the wind
and she felt like she could fly for the first time
That was an entire lifetime ago
Her wings had since been clipped
Her fear of falling killed her need to climb
But today was a new day
She looked out past her tomorrows
As the fire inside her raged
Her memories of feeling free
Fed her need to rise
Days and nights had passed
Darkness her only friend
Now she was the light
Her wings of fire left her hardened heart in ashes
Once again she was free
Soaring above all that held her down
Never again would she be still

Set Me Free

You're more than just the beautiful I call you
You're the razor's edge I slice my fingers on each time I run my hand across your heart
The darkness I find when I dig too deep
The smile that saves me when the rains come and I lose my way
You're my new beginning
My safe zone
Where I can be the scared boy with a broken heart
And the man who knows what true love is
You are the woman I need
And the one I choose to set me free

Untamed Whisper

She's made of runaway wishes and wild flowers
She's a barefoot walk in tall grass
The first smell of summer rain
And a midnight kiss that lingers on your lips long after she's said goodbye
She's everything the world tries to tame but can't

Simple Things

There are moments when the simple things in life are all that's needed. I miss those moments. I miss the closeness. I miss waking up in the middle of the night and feeling you next to me, even miles away. I miss fighting you for the middle spot on the bed and the perfect position to feel you next to me, without losing all circulation in my right arm. I miss having a partner in crime, even if that crime was stealing a few extra minutes from the morning. I miss those moments between 'have a great day' and 'goodnight moon'. I miss the way your lips filled mine as if they were the final two pieces of a puzzle. I miss the way your hands made me feel like I was unstoppable, how the slightest touch lifted me up to the heavens. But most of all I miss you and how you told me 'I love you' a thousand different ways better than anyone else.

Destiny Looking

I was born from the power of the sea
A true child of the universe
Living off the bounty of the land
Gathering my breath from its atmosphere
My stories can all be heard in the wind
The sun, the giver of life
Each star in the sky holding a new tomorrow
The moon serves as my lonesome guide
And you my only wish

Wild Child

She's nothing I need to control.
No rope to hold her gypsy soul
or cage for her wanderlust.
There is no desire to tame her.
She runs wild and free.
And I am left in awe
how her wings seem to always return her to me; the
place she calls home.

Wrong Turn

My mind went missing. At the end of the day, it followed the long winding roads of my past, that lead to nowhere. It picked up pieces I had left behind - long lost memories that were all but gone. I lied there tossing and turning as dawn rose on a new day. When I awoke, I was back where I had left. All my wrong turns had taken me right where I needed to be.

Angels Fall

Angels fall from the diamonds in her eyes,
as she watches her world slip away.
Guilty of love,
sentenced to life without forgiveness.
Her shredded wings clipped, held down by the weight of
a promise that never came.
Only to be set free
by the storm raging inside her
and the tears that washed the lies away.

The Chosen Ones

We were the chosen ones; the poets
Turning life into poems
Embracing the task of taking the shredded pieces from our past and creating a wondrous tapestry to wrap the lost souls in
Giving them a place of shelter from the day

Whiskey Rebound

The whiskey calls your name
As the night asks to stay a little longer
Turn down the lights and let's make this a party
The sound of rolling ice
Cuts through the daydream silence
I am broken in place
Held together by the bottom of this glass
Drink down the settled pieces
Taste my imperfections
and make me whole again

Guardian of Hope

The moon is welcomed each night by the limitless wishes of those who still believe in magic
It shines on the faces of those who cannot see the light during their darkest hours
It harnesses the power of the tide and gives breath to the seas
It sits guarded among the stars cutting a path through the midnight sky that has navigated wayward souls for an eternity

Battle Torn

I often wonder if I've broken the vessel. Is the hardened shell already cracked? Has exposing the soul inside to the ways of this world tainted my inner peace or has it simply allowed me to grow an understanding that we all face this world alone surrounded by countless warriors fighting the same daily battle.

Sweet Hope

I see the broken
The countless lovers caught in a landslide of dying dreams
The misplaced souls that gave up the search mid-journey
Their days not much more than a blur
Their nights filled with wander
Holding on to the glimmer of hope that refuses to die as it guides them through the darkness
A reminder that with time, even the lost, will be whole once again.

Dandelions

Dance among the dandelions but always tread with feathered feet, for they will carry wishes of a better tomorrow come the end of spring.

The Joker

A self proclaimed king
Sits within a glass house upon a throne of lies
ALONE
Like a Joker lost in the deck
His ego filled head adorned by a foil crown of gumballs and plastic hearts
His days of grace long behind him
His destiny being written out before him by the promises of false prophets and hopeless Sirens
He is a ghost of a man
Leading the masses into the darkness where he rules over nothing with a blackened heart

Flames always create the best light in which to navigate

New York Goodbye

I had not seen her since that last day in New York. I had failed to tell her, that when she left, she took my heart with her. How could she know I'd be chasing it ever since? Her smile. Her eyes. How they reminded me of my own lost treasure. Her mouth quivered 'Goodbye' as she turned to kiss me farewell. I was left with the lasting sting of her touch. The longing to be branded by her skin once again. And the never ending memory of how she tastes when my name escapes her lips.

Dark Sanity

I will follow you into the darkness
The ever changing chaos of your mind
And be there
when the screams come
To offer the silence of my sanity
So that you one day can smile
Knowing you are never alone

Sitting With Thought

Sitting behind my desk lost in thought. My fingers glide across the keys like I'm savoring the delicate flesh of an angel. Whether passion or pain, it fills my veins, making its way from my thoughts to the tips of my fingers. And onto the page, the blood spills and my soul is exposed. I am naked for the world to see. The words paint vivid pictures of my ups and downs, my fears and my falls. Connected to those who choose to read them. Every joy I've celebrated is lived out in the imagination of others. Forever leaving a piece of me to hold on to and cherish. Long after this world has proven my mortality, my soul will live on and I will be reborn with every turn of the page.

Heart Light

When you catch it in the right light,
you'll see how each shattered piece of my heart never
truly fit back in place again.

Dance With Chaos

There are days when the peace of mind I celebrate
dances with chaos, leaving my dreams punch drunk,
wishing on coin flips and shooting stars.

The Storm

I am the storm
do not question my might
or the full force of rage
that has kept itself at bay for all these years
dare those who choose to feel the wrath
do not question my purity
for it will cut you clean
and sever the ties that bind
each path traveled has been chosen
forged by the fire inside
the miracle before you
is simply a soul finding its purpose
the cries you hear
are that of a warrior's heart finally weeping
left battle-torn in the aftermath
of what some call heaven

Dear Father

I only knew him as my father but as time has passed, I have learned much more about the man. It wasn't until after he was gone, that I was able to look back on things and understand what a strong and brilliant man he truly was - humble, goodhearted, compassionate to a point and took absolutely no bullshit. He instilled in me that everything has a consequence; good or bad. He wanted me to learn for myself what repercussions came from the decisions I made. Because of that, I was able to learn the ways of the world long before I'd have to put that knowledge to use. My father was a good man and a sometimes know-it-all. How I'd give anything to see him again and let him think he was right just one more time. Don't live with regrets. Don't leave something unsaid. Most of all, never let something petty get in the way of family or friends.

Heaven Sent

*Beneath the shadows
is where she finds me,
the angel I call home
Pulling me to her in the night
I am wrapped safely
in her moonlit wings
The love she gives,
comforts my weary soul,
brings shelter to my dreams,
lighting the darkened rooms
inside my heart*

A Love Story

He had known her for years. Shared minutes of small talk with nothing more than a "hey" or "hello". He had always found her to be beautiful and secretly admired her for longer than he'd like to admit. The moment she walked in the door that night, he saw her as more than a friend. The days of heartache and searching had ended. Neither of them could've imagined just how much that night would come to mean. It changed both of their lives. They knew no matter what happened from that day forward, no one would ever take the others place inside their hearts. The love they shared was one without explanation. It was beyond any man-made label. What had started with a smile, ended with a kiss, that united two souls destined to become one.

Lights in the Night

The sound of her heartbeat drowned out the chaos of my mind. The way my name escaped her lips each morning made the sunrise a second thought. But it was how her skin felt next to mine when our bodies became one in the night, that had me begging the moon to never lose its shine.

Angel's Sin

I have watched angels drown in pools of fire for the sins they have seen, as devils sprout wings and soar to the heavens for committing them.

Never Back

We all will experience loss at some point in our lives. I am sure many of you already have; in some form or another. Don't live with regrets. Don't leave something unsaid and most of all never let something petty get in the way of family or friends. There are days when each step you take feels like the hardest. The most difficult, as if it will all crumble down around you at any moment. On those days - never lose hope or stop dreaming or allowing love into your heart, no matter what. Any direction in life other than backward is a success and should be celebrated as
such.

Celebrate victories but remember each battle.

Silent Suffering

I suffer in silence with the words I never say. The distance between us feeds my desire, leaving me longing for your touch. I find myself envious of the morning sunlight as it kisses your face, welcoming you to another day. How I wish I could stand guard over your dreams at night. I'd sprinkle myself into your every thought and stay there forever.

Kissed Regrets

I have seen you a thousand times with a smile on your face, hiding every mistake you thought you made. And in my dreams, I have kissed away every regret you ever cried.

Thief of Dreams

Hey there little boy
Sitting in your high chair
With an entitled grin and societal exception
You coward
You thief of dreams
Remember her name
Remember her face
She is a survivor; full of strength and dignity
So glad Daddy could hold your hand
and beg for your mercy with the deep pockets of privilege
Lust driven enough to take what you want,
not man enough to face the fire
But you will
The gates of hell will welcome you home one day
How does it feel to rip out someone's soul?

Victories

Let us share our day full of victories
As only lovers can
Under the stars at night
with the heavens as our view
Along the shoreline
as the sea crashes down around us
During a hot Summer night
with fireflies and late night swims
Cherish each ordinary miracle
For today is all we have
Waste it not on wishes for tomorrow

Roots will grow wherever you are.

Surviving the Gone

Through tear stained eyes
I seize the moment
Steal a smile from the mirror
And find my strength
How bittersweet the Springtime is
When life is in bloom
And the heart is in ruin
Every beat takes me further away from paradise
Each morning breaks through with a 'what if'
and the nights end with a 'please stay'
I never knew midnight had a voice
Until I heard the darkness cry your name
How haunting the silence can be
After our song has played
With your ghost not too far behind
I simply survive by dancing alone

Heart and Mind Warrior

*You are my soul's defender
when my heart and mind
wage war against each other.
My sweet surrender anytime
life has been too strong. And
you will be my most cherished
memory when the heavens
come for me at the bitter end.*

Masked Beauty

Your lies and promises were intertwined together. They painted such a beautiful portrait. It looked so glorious shattered across the floor. Each breath filled my lungs with poison and spread your disease. Your love was my death and your departure lit the fire inside. Never again will I be blinded by masked beauty and false hope.

Uncontrollable Force

There are open wounds
that just won't heal
I pour salt onto the scars
And swig down the bitter sweet pain
with a shot of reality

There are words
that can never be unheard
I stab at them with a dull blade
And sing along in harmony
with soulful abandon

There are sights
that cannot be unseen
I wash the slate clean again
And set my sights
with pure intent

There are tastes
that won't ever leave my lips
I curse the heavens
And swallow them down
with a defiant grin

Eternal Echoes

*There are nights
that will never cease to end
I pull the shades on tomorrow
And snuff out each candle
with a cold heartless breath*

*Then there is you
that uncontrollable force
I hold my head high
And beg for mercy
with my heart in my hand*

Broken Cuddles

She made love to my scars and kissed her way through the bitterness, just so she could cuddle with all the broken pieces

Every Chance

Life is short and we are dead a long time. Never get so used to something that we forget how important the little things in life are. Take time to truly live, not simply go through life. Give trust to everyone, until they show reason not to. Don't be fooled by lust or force yourself to love – it should come naturally. And most of all – let the people in your life who mean the most – know they do – EVERY CHANCE YOU CAN because one day you won't have that opportunity.

Smoke Rings

She reads smoke rings from across the bar like they're promises of forever
When will she learn that fifteen minutes of pleasure won't ever soothe the soul
Love is not the boots that sit at the foot of her bed
And the door slamming goodbye will never pick up the pieces of her shattered heart

I have come to realize life is beautiful and at times simple but never easy.

You are not weak

On the days when you're not strong, never feel that you are weak. It's during that time, when things are at their darkest - the love of another will give you the strength to break down your walls.

Be the light

During the nights that you're not brave, never live in fear. Hidden in all the darkness, you will find the light. Loving someone freely will give you the courage to find tomorrow is a brighter day.

Love finds a way

When you don't feel worthy of it, love will always find a way. While you're walking through hell, you will find heaven. It will keep you safe from harm, carry you high and get you home.

On My Way

Struggles, hard times, and sleepless nights
No tea leaves or a crystal ball
Just a heart on my sleeve
Wishing to wake up tomorrow and still believe

Days and nights go by and by
Leaving regrets and smiles just the same
Wishing upon shooting stars
Hoping to be lying right where you are

Tonight the light seems like it's the darkest
The tears of my past taste bitter still
Open the door for another day
Take the next step and I'll be on my way

Tainted

How do I remove your fingerprints from my burning flesh? I have scrubbed and cannot wash it clean, yet I am raw down to the bone. Just as the poison you fed me continues to run through these veins, your tainted love will haunt me to my grave.

A Moment Alone

There isn't a moment alone I have not felt your body next to mine, how I wish you were here to soothe my flesh with your burning touch. The echoes of how my name sounded escaping your lips haunt me, and leave me longing to taste the sweetness of your desire. And as I lie here with only the memories of us, I can't help but come crashing back to the reality that I am alone and lost without you.

Soulshine

How beautiful it is to watch love grow.
How devastating it is to feel love die.
The joys of wonder will bring ordinary miracles to life and the conflicts of self-doubt will cast shadows across the happiest of hearts.
It is then when the soul needs to shine brightest to light the way.

Wicked

We exist in extremely troubling times. Even though the wolf at the door seems relentless, never lose the will to survive. Living with a pure heart gives the soul strength to outlast the wickedness.

Smiles and Daydreams

I want to live my life truly happy. To wake up each morning and face the day with a smile, as if I am living out a daydream. Hard work and sacrifices should be rewarded with a willing heart to share the beating, a gentle touch to soothe the soul, and a soft place to land when the world spins out of control.

Bloom Bright

*I have seen tomorrow bloom bright in your eyes.
Shared a breath with you the moment after a new years sunrise.
Wiped away tears of joy and soothed each others cries.
Now you ask me to believe the lie that this could be our last goodbye.*

All in a Look

There's just something in the way her eyes always find mine, that lets me know I'm hers.
The love
The loyalty
Every piece of herself that she leaves vulnerable, can be felt.
Her dreams and passions,
Her losses and disappointments,
hide in the twinkle.
If you ever need to know true emotion,
it's right there - all in a look.

I'd love to be your Saturday night but long to be your Sunday morning

When I kiss her, it's as if I'm in the perfect storm and I am completely safe.

Sudden Change

There is no manual for navigating through this life.
There's a constant mix of joys,
disappointments, laughter, love, and loss.
The hardest of which,
is the gradual learning that comes after sudden changes.

Chances

We ran aimlessly through this town, taking chances and called it an adventure. We stole kisses under the Friday night bleachers and called it love. It seemed our days were never ending obstacles on our way to wherever the hell we were going. These streets call our name and we owe them everything. Each step we took holds a memory and every forgotten regret a reason why we never busted out.

Take me to where your dreams live, where stardust meets sunlight.

Scattering Ashes

As every grain of sand passed through the hourglass, time seemed to stand still. The memories piled high, only to crash to each side in an uncontrollable slide. My thoughts took me back to a dream I had as a child. I was a lost boy, endlessly searching for my way back home. I had stumbled down a large hill only to find myself grasping at the soil under me, doing all I could to pull myself up and out. The sinking ground around me was burnt moments of my future. The same hands that were just out of reach from helping me get where I needed to be, were scattering ashes, making my ascent even longer. The more time it took me to rise from the depths, the shorter my life became. It took me years to understand what it all meant - Every risk we take can feel like an impossible journey. There will be those who act as if they want you to succeed but would like nothing more than to see you fail. You are responsible for your own actions. No one can travel the path for you. It is up to you to make sense of the twists and turns. Be strong and never give up on your dreams.

Let's Get Wet

As kids, we have no real inhibitions. As we grow older we stop enjoying things the way we once did. We're taught fear, the 'right way to do things' and humility. I used to love running through puddles after a good rain storm, no matter the size. My clothes couldn't soak through fast enough. I still have memories of my grandmother mad as hell because I would walk barefoot everywhere I went during my summers in Florida. There wasn't a challenge I couldn't defeat. Youth isn't wasted on the young, we just allow it to grow old. Somewhere along the line, I stopped coming home drenched. I stopped needing to wash my feet before I walked through the door. I stopped being venturesome. I want that all back. I want to feel the Earth underneath my toes. I want to live and love fearlessly. I want to stand in the middle of a thunderstorm, my head pointed towards the sky, with a smile and a wink as if to say, "Let's get wet!"

4:00 AM

The night is too quiet.
The bed too empty.
4:00 AM is when it starts
the thoughts
the second guessing
wondering what they're doing now.
It's the little things in life that are missed
the companionship
the kisses for no reason
the shared smiles
the laughter.
A partner in crime is hard to come by.
One that understands you,
hurts with you
and hopes with you,
is even more rare.
Cherish the ones you love.
When you find someone that fights for you
and your dreams,
don't allow insignificant instances to create a permanent loss.

Reckless Lust

Desire has a way of dying a slow death. And although a love lost can always be found, the unknown of tomorrow creeps in, pushing the memory of yesterday just out of reach

Darkness Rules

When life is lived always chasing 'the why', there's a certain solace in finding a quiet corner to escape one's own inner thoughts. Hurt takes its toll on the soul. Wisdom offers a deeper kind of pain. It no longer renders one devastated, it's more a profound feeling of disappointment. If each experience is absorbed and internalized, it will create a space within the heart and mind where darkness rules. Do not depend on others to illuminate your days. Become your own shine. Allow the glow from within to light the way out of the shadows.

Coffee Time

There's a moment just after the day breaks which offers an early glimpse of what's to come. In those precious instances, we can elect to embrace all that stands before us or pull and push against it. Each and every day we are given a fresh chance, a blank page to write into history. Choose your memories wisely, because after it's all said and done, they are all we have.

Poison

Each kiss a spell. Every glance, a wish cast into the void as I stand on the edge of tomorrow. My love for her has become as familiar to me as the taste of poison.

Find Your Tribe

*When we truly realize we are not alone, is when we need others the most. We cannot
always fight the world ourselves. Find your tribe and let them in.*

Flying High

*Most times, the journey is often more
important than the destination. Life is
about enjoying the ride. It is important
to remain unpretentious. Your day
doesn't have to be a mad dash to tomorrow. Always take strides to keep going forward but stay focused on what's important. There will be days when you are flying high and others when you can't seem to get your feet off the ground. Enjoy every moment - even those that aren't pleasant - each one will leave a lesson.*

Intoxicating

Her mere presence took my breath away.
The energy just radiated from within.
She was a true force of nature.
A powerful calm in a world full of mayhem.
Her eyes, her smile, her laughter, were all so intoxicating.
Our time was short-lived but the memories are anything but fleeting.

Eenie Meenie

Pick Me! Pick Me! Pick Me! Love cannot be found by swiping right. Cupid doesn't have an email address. Your heart should not be used as a pawn in a fool's game of Eenie Meenie Miney Mo. Never sell it short. True love isn't a game at all - it will never keep score.

Open Up

Fear has kept her from falling so fast.
Her mind has ruled her heart
  since the first day of May when life took its turn. How the road ahead of her suddenly curved and how the door to her past was nailed shut,
sworn to never open up again.

Next Level

Her love was a disease that I wanted no cure for.
Her eyes were the sun that I could not help staring directly into.
Her voice was a lullaby that sang me to sleep
and her smile brought me to the next level of happiness

London Style

Take me to a place where the day breaks for tea and crumpets.
The hustle doesn't come with any bustle and the crowned king is a queen.
I want to live my life London Style.

Enchanted Mist

In the haze of the morning after, my
mind wandered to a better time, when
everything seemed to be much simpler. The world was
ours for the taking. Days were golden and full of glory.
Love stood watch over our souls like a guardian of
dreams. And in that brief moment, I closed my eyes as
the morning fog surrounded me like an enchanted mist
you emerged from. In that instance, my heart began to
beat once again - still broken but beating.

Worthy of Joy

Little by little, we come to realize that as much as we try and mold ourselves into who we want to be, our surroundings and situations win out more times than not. Sometimes in life, we hit hurdles and instead of jumping over them, to stay on our path, we allow them to control the next move. Those choices all come with consequences, both good and bad. There are times when we block our own well-being, simply because we don't feel worthy. The walls of self-doubt can take years to break down. Know that you are worth it and deserving of happiness and more importantly, love. Don't ever lose your joy. Take comfort in the choices you have made, each one has been vital in helping you face the life ahead of you.

Broken Stories

How beautiful the broken stories are my heart tells.
Far more colorful than anything my imagination could
ever dream up.
Reality has a way of painting a vivid picture
and leaving me wanting to know just where the plot
twists take me.
Each page is written as I go, every one revealing itself
line by line.
Bookmarks keep the favorite moments at my fingertips.
But please don't spoil the ending;
There are a few blank pages left to be written before I am
just spilled ink upon a page.

Whenever I hear your name in the wind, my ears know
the same joy my heart felt when it was yours.

Thank you

Thank you for leaving. I learned just how beautiful broken can be and the importance of self-acceptance. My personal happiness is not decided by others. Joy is something I have within me and no one has the power to take it away. Your lies taught me to accept even the darkest of truths. Those same lips that took me to heaven, had the ability to cut me to the core with each unkept promise. Your goodbye set me free. Each day holds an opportunity to find forever. You not fighting to stay showed me how temporary sadness is not a permanent way of life. But more importantly, I finally understood that fate carves its own path and trying to force your will on it, will simply leave you lost. Because of you, I found my way.

Beautiful Tears

The tears just wouldn't come.
No longer would she allow those precious gems to fall.
She knew there would always be ups and downs, good times and bad.
The days ahead were laid out before her and the path looked absolutely beautiful.
Her life was now her own.
Determined to never allow another's unsettled soul to pilfer her joy again.

Roses without thorns; love without loss

Willing Touch

Every heartfelt look, each vibrant smile that crossed her lips, couldn't hide the pain. The memories were just too strong. The emptiness that remained wasn't something that could be occupied with the soft willing touch of a new love. Sometimes the missing pieces of your past, leave holes far too large to ever be filled again.

With love, stone cold hearts melt

Shine on! I will find you.

Comfort and Chaos

The clock ticked away at the madness.
My body and soul had finally become one.
I was no longer lost in the why and what for;
the seemingly timeless chatter between the heart and
mind.
It is there I found the sweet serenity
of questions that have no answers.
The universe with all its wisdom
had surrendered
and I had found my home within the comfortable chaos.

Happy Heart

The happiest of hearts don't always carry the most joy. All too often those who have been shattered before, continue to pump love out to those around them. And although the pieces are never put back together quite the same, the light that still shines is far more beautiful.

Never live without purpose. Rage like a roaring fire, with the control and power of a lover's whisper.

Stardust

She was magic.
The universe had sprinkled stardust across the sky
and where it landed,
formed an unstoppable force.
She was freedom and strength,
mixed with compassion and fire.
She was moonlight.
Her eyes lit up the world
and her voice soothed each broken soul.

No Limits

You are a fool to think there is no limit to the bends a heart will make before it breaks. A beat out of place. A tear down the face and the moment is lost. Wake to a new day and start to heal once again. Let it flutter free and wild and love will find a way.

Night Moves

The day breaks away from a dream.
I am left in limbo with a life not yet lived. Tears stain the sand below,
oceans forming at my feet.
Drowning in the memories;
the lost wishes of when I was young.
My youth is all but gone
and soon the night will make its moves into the twilight of tomorrow.
Where I will remain a simple story,
as my pages turn in the wind.

Secret Whispers

The moment your lips touched mine,
I knew there was no turning back.
We had crossed the line
and each day spent was our way of sharing secret whispers with the world.

Sunset Darkness

The air stings my lungs like breathing in a frosty fire.
My face can feel the days growing colder
as the sunset's darkness arrives far too early for my liking.
The frost turns each window into a picture frame.
Each one holding a new view of a beautiful life.
I love those nights beside you,
when winter comes calling
and how your summer soul forever shines.

Face the Day

Moments caught in time.
Simple memories spread out before me.
Timeless reminders of how life goes on,
even when it feels as if you cannot.
It is only with a caged heart
and ice in my veins,
I am able to face the day
after a night alone with your ghost.

Without passion, everything just seems ordinary.

Time spent with someone is truly never wasted. You will either learn a lesson or create magic.

This One Time

It's not always clear if love will last. But there is a definitive moment in a relationship when it reveals it will not. It hits like an epiphany - an inevitable conclusion many try to ignore in the hopes of saving the heart from being abandoned. It needs to be understood, allowing the heart to beat broken, is much worse than it beating alone.

Forget My Name

My heart,
battle torn and tested,
still beats.
My mind,
tangled and twisted,
still holds memories of a time when all we were was
perfect.
Never forget my name
or the moments we cherished.
Within me a light will always shine,
so the gypsy soul inside of you can find its home.

I am not dead; simply dying because crumpled
daydreams evaporated.

Small Town

I walk the streets of this town and each mile holds a memory.
The roads that pass through are paved with golden smiles and stained with the occasional tear.
I think back on those that couldn't wait to set themselves free from the cage of small town living.
Happy I never took the first step to leave it all behind.
The wings I grew were never meant to fly me away.
My friends have become family and the ties that bind won't ever be severed.
When my days are done, my head will rest under the same ground my feet have roamed.

Wild Ride

There is nowhere to run from the wild ride of living. We are each met with uphill climbs and at times, the hurdles along the way seem insurmountable. No truer statement in regard to life has been made than 'No One Gets Out Alive.' So go on the adventure. Take the nap. Don't be a bully. Eat the cookie. Have cereal for dinner. Sleep past noon on a Sunday. Meet friends for drinks. Kiss the girl or the boy or both. Buy the dress. Visit Paris. Love unconditionally. Tell the truth. Fight for those that cannot fight. Paint. Stand up for what you believe. Write. Sing in the shower and the car and at karaoke. And when you run out of things to do, do them all again. You'll be glad you did.

Childhood Dreams

Childhood dreams play out like cartoons on a Sunday morning - simple and full of meaning. How sad it is when our thoughts meet the reality of life. The innocence of youth and the wonder-filled musings, we so freely shared, are left looking out over a lost horizon. Rainbows no longer hold wishes but become alluring reminders of the beauty left after the rain. We realize that each stone along the journey is a step closer in our search for a higher meaning.

Her kiss tasted like my forever.

Open Door

The beauty of life and love is there is always a chance - an opportunity to make it better - a time to overcome - an open door to happiness, that awaits even the most jagged of hearts. No matter the loss, love will forever find a way. The paths taken, the people met, are all key points along the journey - pivotal moments spent serendipitously searching for the destination.

Leather and Lace

The softness of her skin is only matched by the sharpness of her curves. Her hair falls wildly in place as it cascades across bare shoulders. A lost girl longing to be loved and an unshakable force of a woman taking what is hers. I can feel the uncontrollable desire as her body crashes into mine like a firestorm begging to be tamed. A leather and lace lover hiding behind the shine of hopeful eyes.

Solid Gold

I look in the mirror and miss the innocence that once stared back at me. Where have our yesterdays gone? The golden days of youth sit tucked away in the corners of my mind as still frame memories. Why do we wish away the days and look to turn the pages of our story so quickly? The minutes should be measured by smiles and sorrow ticked away in seconds. If I could, I'd relive them all line by line. Then, each bookmark would hold an unmistakable place in time. Never fail to capture each day and savor the daily miracles - create your own masterpiece without the fear of missing a moment.

Dream Tomorrow

Visions of you have turned from a simple wish
to an undying need.
Tomorrow's dream will never fade,
Instead,
I will use the embers from our burning desire
to light my way with hope once again.
Your hand in my hand,
my lips against your flesh
and the soft whispers of your longing breath
echoing in my ears

The World's Weight

I can't promise you the world. Only that you are mine and I'll be there when the weight of yours feels as if it's on your shoulders.

Lost Moments

Joy, sadness, excitement, and fear are all part of this journey.
Those moments can never be lost if they leave a memory.
Flashes of wonder fill the mind,
allowing the past to remain closer than it actually is.
Snapshots of love shared, tears shed, and a life lived.

My Wish

My wish for you is during your most ominous days, the shadows will hold you close and never let you go. That you find a sparkle in each new breath and know the world would be a much darker place without your light. For even hope can survive inside the slightest of shines.

Insatiable

We're torn to pieces,
without knowing the reasons why.
Left alone in a dream of yesterday,
with no days after or before.
Love always takes a part of you.
Ties aren't ever severed clean.
The scars may heal,
since there's an insatiable need to find its lost beat.
But the heart almost never truly mends
it just learns to set itself ablaze.

Destiny is when two hearts, two minds, and two souls
know the search is over.

Eventually we all face the storm.

Lonesome Highway

Standing tall,
she faced life's lonesome highway.
Like a gunslinger at high noon,
she stared down the barrel of a smoking gun.
All the weak non-believers she had stumbled upon in her
past, fell at her feet in silence.
The lessons were long gone
but the scars that crisscrossed her humble heart,
left an elaborate maze
for those brave enough to seek the treasure she kept
hidden away.

Fancy Wreckage

I wasn't looking to be fixed, for I am not broken.
I am simply tangled in the fancy wreckage of life.
I wanted her to see the jagged edges of the man that I've become,
the beautiful stained soul I was
and to love me for every flaw
to let her whispered touch run along each crack of this caged heart
and understand that purity is most often found in pieces.

Sinking Moon

This love that you envy was stolen from the shadows of a thousand sinking moons. It has become a scarlet letter branded to my chest. Its story is hidden from the sun and tucked away from the world.

Cold Yet Burning

The memory of us is frozen in time.
Simple reminders of a love lost to foolish pride.
We seemed to have it all.
As close to perfection as either of us had been.
The golden ticket.
We had found what so many only dream of.
How quickly it's wiped away.
Now all that's left, are cold sheets and a burning desire to feel the flames one more time.

There's a brief moment just after a storm, that split second before the sun shines and the sky turns clear again. That's what love feels like. It's where love calls home. The infinite space between serenity and chaos.

Where I Belong

There are times when I feel as if each step I've taken on this path is wrong.
That I've somehow forgotten the words to my own song.
The days without you have been nothing but long.
Echoes of the passing hours, haunt me since you're gone.
Alone I stand at the edge and face the dawn.
Wind at my back, sun on my face, hope in my heart -
right where I belong

Knock-Out

The cool morning air filled my lungs with a lasting sting. The sun seemed to wink at me as I tried to clear my head. New beginnings are never easy. I had been knocked down but I'll never be knocked out.

Now or Never

Don't live life with despair but keep in mind, there is nothing wrong with having a bit of a 'now or never' attitude when it comes to living. Days seem to melt into each other and before you know it, another year has passed by - destinations, get-togethers, celebrations, all seem to find their way into hiding. While 60 hour work weeks, bills and worry, grab the spotlight. Responsibilities, of course, need to be met, but what is the cost? Take time to find the balance between work and play. Enjoy the simple things in life. Tomorrow is never guaranteed, so stop making plans to make plans. Life is lived one day at a time, make each one count.

Chasing the Night

Darkness doesn't always find the light.
The sounds of madness were buried deep within and at
times, the only thing that kept me going.
Dancing demons and your ghost,
seem to have me chasing the night.

Eternal Peace

Suffer those who battle love,
for its sword will cut you jagged.
Its blade only meant to bleed you dry.
Left alone, a once noble and beating heart
lies broken and battle torn,
seeking eternal peace at the hands of its captor.

Eternal Echoes

Fuel the Fire

We live in a time that is much different than anything we've ever seen or come to know. Our nation has become separated. We as a whole, need to find a balance once again between taking care of ourselves and having compassion for our fellow man and woman. The only way to do that is to remain steady and stable. If we are to survive as one, each of us has to be self-sufficient and reliable along the journey. Let acceptance and love shine brightly to light the way. Our actions will be the fuel that feeds the fire for change.

Even a wolf needs to rest.

Strange Days

*I have seen rain showers in December
Snow blowing sideways with the wind
I have layed under the stars
As I basked in the crimson light of a blood moon
I have sailed to destinations unknown
Drunkenly sang songs with a room full of strangers
But the strangest of days I've ever known
Are the mornings I wake without you
After the nights you run to me
When he lets you go*

Love without joy is simply wasted.

How High

She wraps all she has to lose inside a broken halo.
Pins all her cares to a wall of dreams with the dagger left in her back.
She sees tomorrow as an escape route from the maze of endless days.
She's high on hope, drunk on love and she's never coming down.

Don't get so lost in the waiting, that you watch someone else go by.

Not Enough

It's not enough to be there every day. She needs to feel it in your kiss. She needs to look in your eyes and know she's still yours; that she still makes your heart flutter, even during the toughest times. It's not enough to say good night at the end of the day. She needs to know it was worth all the day's fight to end it with her. She needs to know that should this be the night she closes her eyes forever, there's a heart that will beat a bit broken and a lost soul who longs to meet her again.

Real Value

So many underestimate the real value of a kiss. From friendship to love, it holds true meaning. The kiss speaks in silence, saying what words cannot.

Every Little Thing

I never took her as a lover,
but on cool summer nights,
I can still smell her sweetness on my skin.
I remember every little thing:
the magic, the mystery,
the way she wouldn't ever say my name.
We never made it to the forever,
although, we shared the laughter and tears that came
with it.

Tissues

A woman shouldn't require a tissue to dry her eyes. She needs a shoulder to lean on, a willing ear to listen and a warrior who will battle those tears.

Dark Angel

Beneath the shadows
is where she finds me,
the angel I call home
Pulling me to her in the night
I am wrapped safely in her moonlit wings
The love she gives,
comforts my weary soul,
brings shelter to my dreams,
lighting the darkened rooms inside my heart

You are a diamond among simple stones; brilliant and full of fire.

Midnight Dancing

The wonder of a midnight kiss is a glorious lie.
The best kiss I ever had
was one I didn't see coming,
one I didn't anticipate with the striking of the clock.
The most memorable kisses
are those that can't tell time
and certainly don't play by any man-made rules.

Neon Glow

Her eyes sparkle to life,
hiding a ghost-filled past.
The neon glow catches her smile,
and forced as it seems,
there's a strength that lies beneath.
For her scars are but beauty marks upon a courageous heart.

Wave

Wave after wave it hit me: the lost years, the memories made and how beautiful it is to know there's more to life than what has happened to you.

Free Yourself

You won't find forgiveness in the shadows of yesterday.
Free yourself from the past behind you,
Breathe in hope
and set sail on your journey,
Treat each today as if it's a new destination;
a moment to make memories.
Learn lessons and carry yourself forward,
through the untroubled vision of tomorrow.

Three Wishes

On these cold winter nights, when the air is bitter and unforgiving, I find myself
reaching across this frigid bed. With closed eyes, I can feel you there, much more real than any dream. Our love could be made daily and in the morning sun, your caress would wake me once again. As I fall into peaceful rest, these wishes will soon be dust, gone for the moment but forever on my mind.

The Wild

The chains of love should never be used as a tool to tame but rather a bond that strengthens in order to share the wild.

Confirm

The racing of my heart, the thoughts I have with each breath, only confirm that love can and will find a way through the darkest of times.

Madness

I look into her eyes and see the madness. It's an all too familiar sight, as I am blessed as well.

What's Next

Any time there is change, there will be panic. Even from
a less than ideal circumstance, the
unknown can appear terrifying. What's next may not be
seen until it arrives, but as long
as there is hope, stability, and solidarity - it won't
matter.

Long Gone

Long gone are the naive days of my youth.
Now forever hangs on the wall with other beautiful
memories, as I live through one TODAY at a time.

Sweet Escape

She is what dreams are made of;
an angel's face, slow dancing with the devil.
She is the glory of my morning.
She is the magic in my moonlight.
My sweet escape.
She is love's first kiss and my heart's last beat.

Break of Dawn

In the silence of the early morning, just before dawn can fully break, I wrap my arms around you, thankful for another day. My soft lips meet the tenderness of your exposed skin. And as I feel your body folding into mine, my hushed whispers fill your ears - 'good morning beautiful, I am so happy to be yours.'

Forgotten Chances

Dance with me along this twisted road of life.
Dip your toes in the deep seas of the unknown and let us live out the dreams we once had.

Possible

And when I look into your eyes, I can't help but wonder how it is possible to feel so
complete, when the road beneath me has always been so fractured.

I Am

I am the last in line of those who tenaciously defied the intolerance of this world before me. Ancestral blood courses through my veins, with love, compassion, and pride. When the night comes for their last breath, I am the legacy that will be left behind to tell their story of strength. With a warrior's cry, I will forge through the uncertainty of tomorrow, honoring them with empathy and grace. For their spirit cannot die until I alone find my chest no longer holds a beat.

And even today the sweetest sound I have ever heard is her saying hello.

Paper Planes

At times, it's as if days are spent with our heads in the clouds. Riding the endless winds of our imagination. Soaring high above the life we live. Like paper planes being blown from place to place, without ever having to leave the ground.

Mental Armor

Life isn't always lived quietly.
There are days it screams, when we are simply seeking whispers.

Change You

There is a moment in all of our lives, that forever changes us. For some, it may come early in the form of childhood tragedy. Others are fortunate enough to elude it far into adulthood. Whether it arrives through simply living life or enduring unimaginable loss, we all experience it. It may not be fully understood at the time, but it becomes a retroactive epiphany, creating an imaginary divide between who we were and who we are. The two are completely different and there is no going back.

And if at night my arms still find you, then the day was worth fighting through.

Come As You Are

Your story doesn't need to be flawless.
The path you took to get here,
doesn't need to be filled with all the right steps.
Just come as you are - with
messy days,
wrong turns,
and
broken pieces.
Perfection is found inside the details.

Game Changer

Some cross paths and call it destiny.
Others talk of tomorrow and call it fate.
I think of forever and call it you.

Show Me

Show me more of what made you.
Don't bring the fancy.
Don't give me veiled tales of bliss.
I want to know how you earned your scars. Tell me what brings you to your knees in the darkness of night.
Peel back the layers.
Let me see the things that make demons run and lesser men hide.

Take Flight

All her shine was hidden in the shadows.
Her heart had beat itself into submission
for far too long.
Each flutter fueled her fear.
Caged behind an open door,
she finally found her wings and took flight.
Now she shimmers among the stars.

The reason why so many never soar is because the only way to fly is to fall.

Find the Way

*During your proudest moments
those days of undeniable strength
When each step you take
raises you above it all
keep an open heart and remember
in your darkest hours
those nights you feel your weakest
when every breath leaves you broken
love will always find a way*

Wide Eyes

With wide eyes,
she seeks a way to navigate through this maze.
The ins-and-outs of life have left her lost.
The years spent in shadows
find her searching for the sun.
And even with broken wings,
she will soar high above the hopes and dreams she's held
captive for all these years.
Her voice will be heard.
Her heart will beat again.

When you're born a dreamer, the mind never truly sleeps.

Footsteps on the Moon

I sit at the edge of this town, with nothing but what's left of forever in front of me.
My gypsy soul wants to run; to love along the way and never look back.
But my grounded heart, with its tangled surrender, keeps me from spreading footsteps on the moon.

Embrace your flaws. You may be weathered and worn, tattered and torn, battered and bruised but you are not broken. Know you've become perfectly imperfect.

Barbarians and Kings

A crown is worthless when made of foil and honored by fools. The throne you sit upon is nothing more than an abandoned home a better man once called his. There is no glory or honor in found fortune and no salvation in stolen joy.

Ravenous

How wonderful this world could be if always looked at through the eyes of a child; ravenous for knowledge, forever ready for
a new adventure. Each day would be filled with honesty and truth. Beauty would be seen in the most innocent and sincere way.
Imagine how simple and carefree life would be, without judgement and without the true understanding of loss.

Lost Hope

There are days when it's as if the moonlight won't ever come.
Each step taken feels like the wrong one.
For these moments of lost hope,
know you are not alone.
And although the setting sun is not your savior,
there are far better days ahead.
For darkness is swift but temporary
and the new dawn brings fresh light.

When All Else Fails

When all else fails, take in all the beauty that surrounds you. Cherish each breath and seize every day as if it's your last. For everything is possible with a heart that is full.

Outside the Window

The windows to your past cannot be the same as those you look out over tomorrow through. Step out from behind the wall. Open the door and let life in. Allow your dreams to roam free and let the magic of wanderlust take your fears on an adventure.

Ashes to Ashes

We welcome the burn of desire;
the fire that rages inside passion.
But no one is ever ready
for the embers that remain when love is lost.
A soul is left to sift through the ashes
until it is blown free by the wind.

Between the raindrops is where the human soul can hide; escaping the world for just a moment.

Afterlife

When my days on this Earth have run out, I am hopeful I will have left memories in minds and given aspirations to dreams. I hope my words have taken breaths away. For I am blessed in sharing the beats of countless hearts. And if you should ever hear my name in passing, please share a smile, so my soul can continue to shine.

Eternal Echoes

Rainbows

Rainbows don't always bring gold.
Just like smiles don't always offer happiness.
We mask our days behind lying eyes
and worn out cliches.
We muffle the screams with laughter,
hide our tears by dancing in the rain
and we call it living.

Winter's Chill

The winter chill has found me once again.
How peaceful the ghosts, who let me toss and turn
without your touch.
And how gently the demons lie beside me during the
darkness.

Silence

In the silence of the early morning dawn, lost souls seize the few remaining moments of the night. Hidden hopes and misplaced dreams fill their pockets with foolish pride. One by one the moon collects their wishes as they seek shelter from the sun's shadow once again.

Even the saddest poetry is made beautiful because tears and blood mix to make the perfect ink.

Begin Again

I crave the softness of your kiss
Begging to feel your tender mercy
as I face my sins
I want to fulfill each promise
you ever made to yourself
Longing to see the beauty that hides behind your smile
Your love has been kept from the world
far too long
Stuff your doubts deep down within
Unleash the river of tears
that led you back to me
and never allow them to fall again
For you are my strength
My long lost half
The end of my beginning

The Haunt

There isn't a moment alone
I have not felt your body next to mine,
how I wish you were here
to soothe my flesh with your burning touch
The echoes of how my name sounded
escaping your lips haunt me,
and leave me longing to taste the sweetness of your
desire
And as I lie here with only the memories of us,
I can't help but come crashing back to the reality
that I am alone and lost without you.

Our yesterdays are lessons for tomorrow.

No Worries

I haven't thought about 'what if' in a long time but you've got my mind wishing miles weren't worries and that distance could be traveled in the blink of an eye. My mind wanders to think just how beautiful the sun shining through these windows would look on your face. I long to believe your feet could call this space home and how easy Sunday morning would be with your heart keeping its beat next to mine.

Sometimes the best paths we take are wrong turns.

Ever After

My smile sought shelter
Falling through the cracks
of lost broken dreams
Until it landed
on the beat of my heart
and they lived
happily ever after

From Under

You lit my yesterdays
with your endless smile
Made wishes upon stars
And cast them out into the night
Like love sick diamonds to light our way
Find me there under them now.
When your days have left you weary,
my heart will always be your home
and my lips will forever call your name

Into the Fire

My days are spent walking in the fire.
Sifting through the ashes of days gone by.
My past barely recognizable,
smoldering under foot.
Bury the memories,
for they have burned long enough.
Time has come to forge a new path
and set my future ablaze.

Cage

Calling your name in the night
Like a love howl offered to the moonlight
This heart beats alone in a cage
Fueled by passion and rage
Needing you its only crime
The sentence handed down - a lifetime

Lost Whispers

*How strong the bonds are that remain
when shared wishes become found dreams in the silence
of a lover's kiss.
Like an angel at dawn,
her warm breath would wake me to a new day.
Those precious memories
have left me with a hopeful heart.
But lost are the whispers
that came in the night.
Life's soft reminders
of just how fragile love is.*

Nights Echo

Through the darkness
an echo pierces the silence of the night.
A howl so fierce
even the shadows part their ways
And as the dawn breaks
The moon will try desperately to hide its face away from the sun
In the end, this warrior's call
will allow my pack to rest

Speak Again

Tell me again about true love; how it doesn't run and doesn't hide. Then tell me again why you spent your days in the silence of shadows and were gone long before the goodbye.

The unknown is no place for the heart to remain.

Do Not Disturb

Do not disturb old feelings once they have found their final resting place. They were buried for good reason; the damage was done. You can't allow yourself to be pulled down the same path once again. Life cannot be fully lived when the past is still part of your future. Let the memories that remain lie where you left them.

Green

*Like the first green buds of Spring,
love seems to blossom as it grows.
How important it is to handle the soul with care, as each
day is vital in strengthening its roots. Take time to
nurture with a gentle touch and
just watch how it blooms.
For the warmth of a day spent in the heart
of another brings new meaning to life.*

May the stars remember your wishes and the heavens grant each one.

Inside the Fire

I found myself standing inside the fire. Endlessly
searching the depths of my existence.
The flames fanned by self-doubt and countless lost
dreams.
But with a warrior's call,
I stand at the edge of tomorrow,
my heart full of hope
and my past left in the ashes.

Lost Garden

There's a lost garden deep within my soul.
Where dreams and wishes long to bloom.
During moments of doubt, I bask in the bliss of the hope
it bears. When fear and doubt fall too close to the vine,
there's comfort in knowing each new dawn brings me to
you.

Forever Wild

Do not try to tame what was born free.
A cage is no place to realize your dreams. Being chained in place is not considered living.
Allow your wings to ride the wind and stay forever wild.

Open Road

Along a lost highway is where you'll find me when my days meet their end. Life's happiness is not discovered in a single destination but rather the journey we set out on. The open road between one point and another is where lessons are learned and memories made.

What Happens Now

What happens when the truths become lies? When the pieces of the past start to crumble away, revealing a maze of tangled paths you don't recognize.
What happens when the voice of reason
suddenly fuels your doubt?
Do you question all that has lead you to this place?
Can you ever truly trust anything from this day forward?
How do you bury the past?
There are no flames worthy enough to
engulf a lifetime of deceit; pride will certainly take care of that.

Only You

She walks through the darkness.
Parting the shadows
as monsters fall at her feet.
And although alone she stands,
she is not lonely.
For the moon rises to light her path
and the night calls her its home.

Heartstrong

Life is fragile. But a lover's heart may be the most resilient part of anyone who dares expose it for another. Break it open - each scar will tell a story of love lost, every beat will hold a midnight kiss, and the pieces will all ache to be whole once again.

Even all of her swallowed tears could not put out the fire
inside.

Next Stop

Where do we go from here?
Flames have reached the bridge.
All the coins have been collected from the
fountain.
You keep me hanging on to your every word
as if the testament to our existence will somehow save
me from the gone in your goodbye.

Nobody's Fool

The midnight sun is suffocated by days of darkness.
Cure the sickness by feeding it poison.
The devil sits laughing,
as you lie drowning in tears of self-pity.
Summon the demons to do the dirty work
and fill the void with emptiness.
For you are nobody's fool but your own.

Thunder

How liberating it is to dance in the rain, to find solace in
watching nature's spectacular
light show paint itself across the sky. But never turn to
run from the thunder; it is a
necessary reminder that beauty needs balance and
freedom still holds fear.

Lucky Find

We all seem to be searching for the proverbial safe place to land. A refuge where laughter and love can live alongside disappointment and hurt, without judgement. As loving individuals, we long
to find those that will complete us. When the one your heart beats for is the same soul your mind dreams of running to, do not minimize the harmony by calling it luck. Know you are truly blessed.

Unwrapped Soul

The unwrapped soul uncovers the purest of truth. It gives strength through vulnerability, allowing it to live life and not just simply exist, but to fully experience each as it is revealed and survive all it has to offer.

Blind Touch

In the depths of the night,
long after I am gone,
look for me in the moonlight.
You'll find me there
in the shimmering tail of a shooting star.
Alone on a summer night, know I'm beneath the blind touch of a warm breeze.
My soul will be seen in the first hint of sunlight, just before dawn, and I will watch over you the whole day through.

You are never truly lost if each step you take is towards home.

A Little Jay on Jay

I am a New York based writer and poet. I grew up in the awe inspiring Hudson Valley area, 60 miles from the greatest city in the world and smack dab in the middle of tranquility and grace. I have had a passion for writing since I was a small child. Being near the Hudson River and water has always helped me find my voice. I find clarity there and a simple no cost way to re-align when things get a bit askew.

Since I can remember, I have loved to write and tell stories. There has always been something special about pen and paper. As a child I remember sitting next to my mother with a yellow legal pad and black felt pen mimicking her cursive writing. Even today I prefer writing by hand to electronic means. I keep a spiral notebook in each room for anytime an idea may arise.

My love for words started when I discovered music. As a teenager anytime I'd get a new album, I'd immediately open up the lyric sheet to read the words even before I listened to the song. As you read in the introduction, my love of poetry began after reading Robert Frost's 'The Road Not Taken' in my college English class. It truly changed my life, as I felt I had always carved my own path, even at a young age.

At age 23 I wrote my first screenplay titled Ashes to Ashes, about a police officer who enlists the help of a close friend to create a drug empire after his partner was gunned down during a drug raid. While I had no real knowledge of how to market my work, and living on the east coast, I tried a few query letters and continued to write. That same year I started writing my second screenplay, but as life and responsibility took over, I put my writing to the back burner and changed my priorities until recently. In December of 2013, I created a Facebook page to share my writing. Since that time, the Writer Jay Long page has attracted thousands of fans.

Story telling, and expressing feelings through words are what I am best at. There is nothing like having someone use my words to help heal. Writing allows for the 'perfect' ending to any situation.

I enjoy connecting with fans and sharing pieces of myself with the world. I am following my dreams and traveling down a path that was laid out many

years ago. I love hearing that others connect and can relate to my writing. I hope you follow me on one of or all of my social media accounts. I try and deliver more writing each day, as well as, recorded spoken versions of my more
popular pieces.

Jay Long

Website : JayLongWrites.com
Facebook: WriterJayLong
Instagram: WriterJayLong
Twitter: JayLongWrites
YouTube: Jay Long Poetry
Pinterest: JayLongWrites
Tumblr: WriterJayLong
Email : jaylongwrites @ gmail.com

To follow my story and continue to support indie artists like myself.
Please visit: patreon.com/jaylong

Please leave a review of this book on Amazon.com and GoodReads.com

Eternal Echoes

www.ingramcontent.com/pod-product-compliance
Lightning Source LLC
Chambersburg PA
CBHW020618300426
44113CB00007B/687